Venite exultemus Domino

for SATB chorus and organ

CHESTER MUSIC

Published by

Chester Music
part of The Music Sales Group
14-15 Berners Street, London W1T 3LJ, UK

Exclusive Distributors:
Music Sales Limited
Distribution Centre, Newmarket Road,
Bury St Edmunds, Suffolk IP33 3YB, UK

Music Sales Corporation
257 Park Avenue South, New York,
NY 10010, USA

Music Sales Pty Limited
20 Resolution Drive,
Caringbah, NSW 2229, Australia

Order no. CH76571
ISBN: 978-1-84938-703-3
© 1983 by The Britten Estate Ltd
Worldwide publication rights licensed
to Chester Music Limited, 2009
All Rights Reserved

Unauthorised reproduction of any part of this
publication by any means including photocopying
is an infringement of copyright.

Cover design by Ruth Keating

Printed in the EU

The right of Benjamin Britten to be identified as the composer of the musical work entitled *Venite exultemus Domino* is hereby asserted. The name of Benjamin Britten as composer must therefore be stated in association with any performances, recording or other use of the Work or any part of it. Any derogatory treatment of this work is illegal. No arrangement of adaptation of this work may be made without the prior written permission of the publishers. Permission to perform this work in public must be obtained from the society duly controlling performing rights unless there is a current licence for public performance from such society in force in relation to the premises at which the performance is to take place. Such permission must be obtained in the UK from The Performing Right Society Ltd., 29-33 Berners Street, London WIP 4AA.

www.chesternovello.com

S.A.T.B.

VENITE EXULTEMUS DOMINO

BENJAMIN BRITTEN
(1913–76)

© 1983 by The Britten Estate Ltd
Worldwide publication rights licensed to Chester Music Ltd, 2009

Venite Exultemus Domino

Venite Exultemus Domino

*C in manuscript

Venite Exultemus Domino

This *Venite*, found among his unpublished works after Britten's death, was evidently composed at the same time as his *Jubilate Deo* in C major, written in 1961 at the request of H.R.H. The Duke of Edinburgh for St. George's Chapel, Windsor. (The *Jubilate Deo* itself was composed as a companion piece to the *Te Deum* in C major dating from 1934, which had been written for Maurice Vinden and the Choir of St. Mark's, North Audley Street, London.) In the *Venite* the tempo indication at the start is editorial, as are a few cautionary accidentals.